Virginia

BY ANN HEINRICHS

Content Adviser: Letitia McManus, Children's Librarian, Richmond (Va.) Public Library

Reading Adviser: Dr. Linda D. Labbo, Department of Reading Education, College of Education, The University of Georgia

COMPASS POINT BOOKS 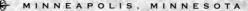 MINNEAPOLIS, MINNESOTA

Compass Point Books
3722 West 50th Street, #115
Minneapolis, MN 55410

Visit Compass Point Books on the Internet at *www.compasspointbooks.com*
or e-mail your request to *custserv@compasspointbooks.com*

Photographs ©: Unicorn Stock Photos/Richard Gilbert, cover, 1; PhotoDisc, 3, 21, 40, 43 (top), 47;
Rob & Ann Simpson/Visuals Unlimited, 4, 6, 42, 47; Robert McCaw, 7, 46 (middle left); Tom Till, 8;
Hulton/Archive by Getty Images, 9, 16; Arthur Gurmankin/Mary Morina/Visuals Unlimited, 11; Unicorn
Stock Photos/Rob & Ann Simpson, 12; Photo Network/Jeff Greenberg, 13, 20, 31; North Wind Picture
Archives, 14; Stock Montage, 15, 17, 19, 23, 24, 41, 44, 45; James P. Rowan, 18, 48 (top); Digital
Stock, 25; Unicorn Stock Photos/Jeff Greenberg, 26; Jeff Greenberg/Visuals Unlimited, 27; Ken
Martin/Visuals Unlimited, 28; Lynda Richardson/Corbis, 29; Getty Images Sport Services, 32; Audrey
Gibson/Visuals Unlimited, 33; Photo Network/Michael Philip Manheim, 34; Photo Network/D & I
MacDonald, 35; Mark E. Gibson/Visuals Unlimited, 37; DigitalVision, 38, 42; Dave Spier/Visuals
Unlimited, 39; Robesus, Inc, 43 (state flag); One Mile Up, Inc., 43 (state seal); Photo Network/Gay
Bumgarner, 46 (top left).

Editors: E. Russell Primm, Emily J. Dolbear, and Catherine Neitge
Photo Researcher: Svetlana Zhurkina
Photo Selector: Linda S. Koutris
Designer: The Design Lab
Cartographer: XNR Productions, Inc.

Library of Congress Cataloging-in-Publication Data

Heinrichs, Ann.
  Virginia / by Ann Heinrichs.
      v. cm. — (This land is your land)
Includes bibliographical references (p.   ) and index.
Contents: Welcome to Virginia!—Mountains, valleys, and shores—A trip through time—Government
by the people—Virginians at work—Getting to know Virginians—Let's explore Virginia!—Glossary—
Did you know?—At a glance—Important dates.
  ISBN 0-7565-0310-8
  1. Virginia—Juvenile literature. [1. Virginia.] I. Title.
  F226.3 .H45 2002
  975.5—dc21   j 917.55   2002002964

© 2003 by Compass Point Books

Printed in the United States of America.

Table of Contents

▲ **Virginia's Shenandoah National Park**

"Give me liberty or give me death!"

Those are the famous words of Patrick Henry. In 1775, he called on Virginians to fight for their freedom from Britain.

Virginia is known as the birthplace of the nation. Many brave Virginians helped create the United States. One was Patrick Henry. Another was Thomas Jefferson. He wrote the Declaration of Independence. George Washington of Virginia was the first president of the United States.

Many favorite stories take place in Virginia, too. One tells about Pocahontas, the daughter of a Native American chief. She was a special friend to Virginia's early settlers. Another favorite story tells about a wild pony named Misty. She had many adventures on Chincoteague Island in Marguerite Henry's *Misty of Chincoteague* books.

Now come and explore Virginia. You'll find it's a very special place!

Mountains, Valleys, and Shores

▲ Virginia's Cape Henry is on the Atlantic Ocean.

Virginia is a land of mountains, valleys, and seashores. Its east coast faces the Atlantic Ocean and Chesapeake Bay. To the northeast is the state of Maryland. West Virginia lies to the northwest. North Carolina and Tennessee run along the south. Southwest Virginia shares a border with Kentucky. The nation's capital—Washington, D.C.—stands at Virginia's northeast corner.

Eastern Virginia is called the Tidewater. Many rivers rush

▲ **Black bears live in parts of Virginia, especially in the Great Dismal Swamp.**

through the Tidewater into Chesapeake Bay. When the **tides** rise, the rivers swell higher. Much of the Tidewater is swampy. Bobcats and bears find a safe home near the southern border in the Great Dismal Swamp.

The Potomac River forms Virginia's northeastern border with Maryland. It flows into Chesapeake Bay. This bay is rich with oysters, crabs, and clams. Virginia has passed laws that keep its waters clean.

Across Chesapeake Bay is the Delmarva **Peninsula.** Three states own a piece of it—Delaware, Maryland, and Virginia. "Delmarva" comes from the letters of each state's name. The peninsula's southern tip belongs to Virginia. It's called the Eastern Shore.

Assateague and Chincoteague are two islands that lie off the Eastern Shore. Wild ponies run free on Assateague Island. Some people believe the first ponies came from Spanish ships

▲ **A wild pony eats grass.**

▲ A 1796 drawing of Richmond

in the 1500s. Other people think they are probably the offspring of ponies set free by early settlers.

The Piedmont Plateau runs down the center of the state. Its steep eastern edge is called the Fall Line. The Tidewater's rivers plunge over the edge in sparkling waterfalls. Early settlers could not get past the Fall Line. They settled there and built Alexandria and Richmond. Richmond became the state capital.

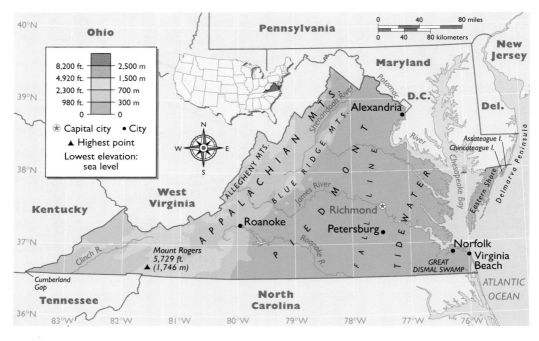

▲ **A topographic map of Virginia**

    The mountains that cover western Virginia are part of the great Appalachian Ridge and Valley region. Much of this beautiful area is protected land. It lies within Thomas Jefferson National Forest, George Washington National Forest, and Shenandoah National Park.

    The Blue Ridge Mountains rise up from the Piedmont. They look out over the rolling hills of the Shenandoah Valley. The Allegheny Mountains form Virginia's western border.

▲ Apple Orchard Falls in Thomas Jefferson National Park

▲ Raccoons live in Virginia's many forests.

As early settlers headed west, these mountains were in the way. At last the settlers got through a break in the mountains in Virginia's southwest corner. That mountain pass is known as the Cumberland Gap.

Forests cover more than half of Virginia. Deer, foxes, chipmunks, and raccoons scurry through them. Quails and wild turkeys rustle about on the forest floor.

Virginia's climate varies from one region to another. On the coast, the weather is mild. The mountains get the coldest winters and the most snowfall. Even in summer, the mountains are cool. When autumn comes, colorful leaves brighten the mountainsides.

▲ A colorful autumn view in Green Cove

Thousands of Native Americans once lived in Virginia. The Powhatan lived all along the coast. They were named for Powhatan, their powerful chief. High log fences surrounded some of their villages. Their longhouses had roofs of bark or reeds. The men hunted wild animals in the forests. Women raised corn, beans, squash, and tobacco.

In 1606, Captain John Smith sailed from England with a group of settlers. They set up the Jamestown **colony** in 1607. This was America's first English settlement.

The **colonists** lived through many hard times in their new home. That first winter, many of them died. Chief Powhatan's daughter Pocahontas often brought gifts of food. Indians also taught the settlers to grow

▲ **Captain John Smith helped settle the Jamestown colony.**

▲ **Pocahontas**

tobacco. It became Virginia's major crop.

In 1619, Virginians formed the House of Burgesses. This group ruled and managed the colony.

In time, thirteen English colonies were developed along the coast. But many of the colonists began to wish for the freedom to rule themselves. In 1775, the Revolutionary War broke out.

▲ **Thomas Jefferson wrote the Declaration of Independence in 1776.**

Thomas Jefferson wrote the Declaration of Independence. Another Virginian, George Washington, led the Continental army. The fighting ended in 1781 with the Battle of Yorktown. A peace treaty was signed in Paris in 1783. The colonists had won their freedom!

James Madison of Virginia helped write a list of basic laws for the new United States. This became the U.S. **Constitution.** Virginians accepted the Constitution in 1788, and Virginia became the tenth state. Soon George Washington was chosen to be the nation's first president.

Slaves worked on Virginia's many **plantations.** Some slaves were treated well, but many were not. A slave named

▲ In 1831, Nat Turner led a slave revolt.

Nat Turner led a **revolt** against whites in 1831. The problem of slavery led to the Civil War (1861–1865).

Virginia and other Southern states soon seceded, or pulled out of the Union. They formed the Confederate States of America. But farmers in western Virginia didn't want to secede. They set up their own state—West Virginia.

Once the war began, Richmond became the Confederate

▲ Visitors to Chancellorsville Battlefield can see original weapons from the Civil War.

capital. General Robert E. Lee of Virginia led the Confederate army. Confederates won important battles at Bull Run (Manassas), Fredericksburg, and Chancellorsville. In the end, however, the Confederacy lost the war. General Lee surrendered at Appomattox Court House in 1865.

By the 1880s, Virginia was a strong industrial state. New factories made ships, cotton cloth, and cigarettes. Farmers were growing much more than just tobacco, too. They raised cattle, apple trees, and many kinds of vegetables.

In the 1930s, the nation was hit hard by the Great Depression. Many Virginians lost their homes and jobs. But things improved after World War II (1939–1945). Shipbuilding became an important industry in Hampton Roads. New government offices and military bases opened.

▲ **Tobacco has been an important crop in Virginia for centuries.**

▲ **A farmer in Charles City checks his cotton crop.**

Today, Virginia is growing faster than ever. Its offices, factories, and farms are busy. Virginians have an exciting past. They also look forward to a bright future!

Government by the People

▲ Virginia's capitol in Richmond

Virginia's proper name is the **Commonwealth** of Virginia. A commonwealth is a government elected by the people. The people and government are united to work for the good of all.

Virginia has three branches of state government—

executive, legislative, and judicial. Having three branches means that no one branch of government becomes too powerful. Richmond is Virginia's capital city.

The executive branch carries out the state's laws. Virginia's governor heads the executive branch. Voters elect a governor every four years. The governor can serve only one term at a time. Governors wanting a second term must wait four years and run again. Many other executive officers help the governor.

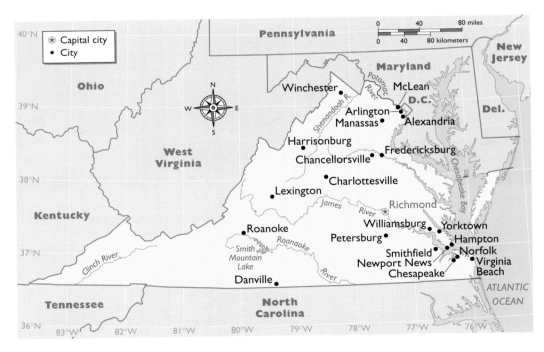

▲ **A geopolitical map of Virginia**

▲ Members of Virginia's General Assembly discuss an issue in 1660.

The legislative branch makes the state laws. State law-makers serve in Virginia's General Assembly. This is the oldest lawmaking body in the United States. It grew out of the 1619 House of Burgesses. The General Assembly has two houses, or sections. They are the forty-member Senate and the one hundred-member House of Delegates.

Virginia's judges make up the judicial branch. They

▲ Fifth U.S. president James Monroe was born in Virginia.

decide whether the law has been broken. Virginia's highest court is the Supreme Court of Virginia.

Virginia is divided into ninety-five counties. Each county has its own government. Virginia has forty independent cities. The people who live there elect their own city governments. Towns with at least 5,000 people can choose to become cities and elect their own city governments.

Virginia is sometimes called the Mother of Presidents. Eight U.S. presidents were born there. They are George Washington, Thomas Jefferson, James Madison, James Monroe, William Henry Harrison, John Tyler, Zachary Taylor, and Woodrow Wilson.

▲ **The Central Intelligence Agency is located in McLean.**

Many national government offices are located in Virginia. The Pentagon is in Arlington County. It houses the U.S. Department of Defense. McLean is the home of the Central Intelligence Agency (CIA). It gathers information to keep the country safe.

Virginia's most important business is government. About one of every seventeen Virginia workers has a government job. Many of them work in U.S. government offices. Others work at military bases.

Tobacco became Virginia's major crop in the 1600s. It's still important today. However, Virginia farmers raise a number of crops and farm animals now. Many visitors to Virginia hope to bring home a Virginia ham. They say the best hams come from hogs in Smithfield. Farmers in the Shenandoah Valley have huge turkey farms. Apple and peach trees grow in the valley, too.

Farms on the Eastern Shore raise chickens, dairy cows, and vegetables. Fishing is also

▲ A North American wild tom turkey from the Yorktown Victory Center in Virginia

▲ A fisher cleans a catch along Virginia's Lynnhaven Inlet.

important along the Eastern Shore. The coastal waters abound with oysters, scallops, soft-shelled crabs, and fish.

Shipbuilding is a big industry in Virginia. Newport News has one of the world's largest shipyards, where ships are built. Virginia's chemical factories make plastics, artificial fibers, and drugs. Northern Virginia is a center for computer and communication companies. These companies serve many national government offices. Virginians make cloth, furniture, and electrical equipment, too.

▲ **A coal mine in Appalachia**

The state has rich deposits of coal in mines in the southwest. Limestone is found in the Shenandoah Valley. Many caves there are hollowed out of limestone. Virginia is the only state that mines kyanite. This mineral is used to make bricks.

Today's Virginians have roots in many **cultures.** Some are the descendants of Virginia's English settlers. Others are descended from Scotch-Irish and German people. They traveled from Pennsylvania to the Shenandoah Valley in the 1700s. Today, almost three out of four Virginians have European **ancestors.**

By the 1860s, about one-third of Virginians were black slaves. Today only about one of every five Virginians is

▲ **A teacher shows children how to care for potato plants at the Lewis Ginter Botanical Garden in Richmond.**

African-American. Many Vietnamese people now live in northern Virginia. Norfolk has a large Filipino community. People from many nations live in the Washington, D.C., area.

In 2000, there were 7,078,515 people living in Virginia. That made it twelfth in population among all the states. More than two of every three Virginians live in or near cities. Northern and eastern Virginia are the most crowded areas. Virginia Beach is Virginia's largest city. Next are Norfolk, Chesapeake, and Richmond.

The Shenandoah Apple Blossom Festival is one of Virginia's most celebrated events. It is held in May, when pink blossoms cover the apple trees. People flock to Winchester for parades, music, and flower-gazing. Another springtime event is Historic Garden Week in April. Visitors may tour hundreds of historic homes and gardens.

Jamestown Landing Day in May celebrates Virginia's birth as a colony. Many activities take place at the Jamestown Settlement. September's Neptune Festival is sand-castle time at Virginia Beach. People compete to see who can build the biggest sand castle.

▲ The seashore in Virginia Beach, the state's largest city

Thousands of people watch the Pony Penning at Chincoteague Island in July. Wild ponies swim across the shallow water from Assateague Island. Then they are sold on Chincoteague. This event keeps the herd from growing too large.

▲ **Mark Carrier of the Washington Redskins signs his autograph for fans in 2000.**

Virginia sports fans cheer for the Washington Redskins. The Redskins don't exactly belong to Virginia! They are the professional football team of Washington, D.C.

The Hokies are a favorite college football team. They play for Virginia Tech, or the Virginia Polytechnic Institute and State University. The Norfolk Tides are Virginia's minor-league baseball team. The best Tides players move up to join the New York Mets.

▲ **The College of William and Mary is in Williamsburg.**

Virginia has many famous schools. The College of William and Mary is the second-oldest college in the United States. (Harvard University is the oldest.) William and Mary opened in 1693 in Williamsburg. Another well-known school is the University of Virginia in Charlottesville. Thomas Jefferson founded it in 1819.

▲ **Men dressed as soldiers stand ready at Colonial Willamsburg.**

What was it like to be a Virginia colonist? You'll find out at Colonial Williamsburg. It has been rebuilt to look just as it looked in colonial times. Its programs re-create the exciting times before independence. Nearby is Yorktown Victory Center. Its costumed soldiers show how the Revolutionary War was fought.

You can watch history unfold before your eyes at Jamestown. It's the site of the first English settlement in

▲ **Houses in James Fort at Jamestown Festival Park**

America. Scientists are at work every day digging up things the settlers left behind.

Would you like to explore the inside of a bubble or the surface of the moon? You can do it all at the Children's Museum in Portsmouth. You can also climb a rock wall or see thousands of toy train cars.

In Richmond you can tour the modern capitol. Nearby is the old Confederate capitol. It is now a museum covering Virginia's Confederate days. Close to Charlottesville is Monticello, Thomas Jefferson's home.

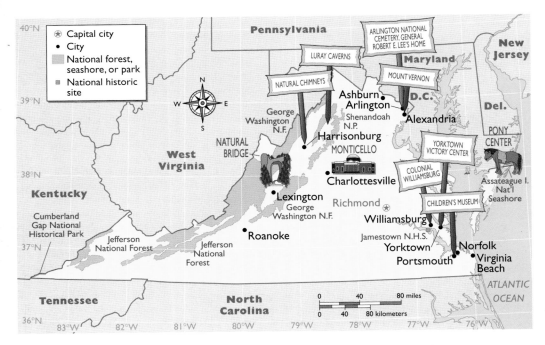

▲ **Places to visit in Virginia**

Arlington and Alexandria are very close to Washington, D.C. More than 200,000 U.S. soldiers are buried in Arlington National Cemetery. President John F. Kennedy's tomb is there, too. One part of the cemetery is General Robert E. Lee's home.

▲ **Arlington National Cemetery**

Mount Vernon, George Washington's home, is near Alexandria. Many famous Civil War battlefields are in this area. They are now educational military parks.

▲ **Mount Vernon was George Washington's home.**

▲ **The underground caves at Luray Caverns have interesting mineral deposits.**

Are you good at solving problems? Then the Garden Maze at Luray Caverns is the place for you! Try to find your way through the **maze** of tall hedges. It takes forty correct choices to succeed. Good luck! But don't miss the awesome underground caves.

Many other cave sites are in the Blue Ridge and Shenandoah Valley region. Another natural wonder in this area is Natural Bridge near Lexington. Natural Chimneys near Harrisonburg are towering, castle-like rocks.

Down in Virginia's southwest corner is the historic Cumberland Gap. Men, women, and children settlers marched through this mountain pass. They were full of dreams about their new life.

As you can see, Virginia is a great place to explore!

▲ **Natural Bridge near Lexington**

Important Dates

1607 The Jamestown colony is founded.

1619 The Virginia House of Burgesses meets for the first time.

1693 The College of William and Mary is founded in Williamsburg.

1776 Thomas Jefferson writes the Declaration of Independence.

1781 The Battle of Yorktown ends the Revolutionary War.

1788 Virginia becomes the tenth state.

1819 Thomas Jefferson founds the University of Virginia in Charlottesville.

1831 Nat Turner leads a slave revolt.

1861– 1865 Virginia fights for the Confederacy in the Civil War.

1863 West Virginia is formed from the western part of Virginia.

1870 Virginia rejoins the Union.

1969 Virginia elects its first Republican governor since 1869.

1989 Virginia governor L. Douglas Wilder becomes the country's first African-American governor.

Glossary

ancestors—a person's grandparents, great-grandparents, and so on

colonists—people who settle a new land for their home country

colony—a territory that belongs to the country that settles it

commonwealth—a government by the people for the good of all

Constitution—a written document explaining the basic laws of the United States

cultures—groups of people who share beliefs, customs, and way of life

maze—a puzzle with a path that has many ways to turn

peninsula—a piece of land almost completely surrounded by water

plantations—large farms worked by laborers who lived there

revolt—an uprising by people who are unhappy with their rulers

tides—the daily rising and falling of the ocean level

Did You Know?

★ Chincoteague Island has an oyster museum.

★ More than half of all Civil War battles were fought in Virginia.

★ Virginians planted the country's first peanuts.

★ Colonial Williamsburg is the nation's largest outdoor living history museum.

★ Four of the country's first five presidents were Virginians.

★ Virginia was named for England's Queen Elizabeth I. She was called the Virgin Queen because she was not married.

★ Virginia is sometimes called the Mother of States. All or part of eight states were formed from territory that once belonged to Virginia. They are Illinois, Indiana, Kentucky, Michigan, Minnesota, Ohio, West Virginia, and Wisconsin.

State capital: Richmond

State motto: *Sic Semper Tyrannis* ("Thus Always to Tyrants")

State nickname: Old Dominion

Statehood: June 25, 1788; tenth state

Area: 42,326 square miles (109,624 sq km); **rank:** thirty-fifth

Highest point: Mount Rogers, 5,729 feet (1,747 m)

Lowest point: Sea level

Highest recorded temperature: 110°F (43°C) at Columbia on July 5, 1900, and Balcony Falls on July 15, 1954

Lowest recorded temperature: −30°F (−34°C) at Mountain Lake Biological Station on January 22, 1985

Average January temperature: 36°F (2°C)

Average July temperature: 75°F (24°C)

Population in 2000: 7,078,515; **rank:** twelfth

Largest cities in 2000: Virginia Beach (425,257), Norfolk (234,403), Chesapeake (199,184), Richmond (197,790)

Factory products: Tobacco products, food products, chemicals, transportation equipment

Farm products: Tobacco, beef cattle, chickens, hogs, turkeys, milk, corn, soybeans

Mining products: Coal, sand, gravel

State flag: Virginia's state flag shows the state seal on a field of dark blue.

State seal: Virginia's state seal shows Virtus, the Roman goddess of virtue. She holds a spear and sword. One foot is on Tyranny, who lies on the ground. Below is the state motto, *Sic Semper Tyrannis*. It is Latin for "Thus Always to Tyrants." It means that good citizens defeat cruel rulers. The picture is about the state motto.

State abbreviations: Va. (traditional); VA (postal)

Arthur Ashe (1943–1993) was a tennis star. He won the Wimbledon and U.S. Open titles. He also played on the winning U.S. Davis Cup team.

Pearl Bailey (1918–1990) was a singer and actress. She starred in the stage show *Hello, Dolly!* and the movie *Porgy and Bess.*

Ella Fitzgerald (1918–1996) was a jazz and blues singer. She was widely loved for her rich voice and her lively style.

William Henry Harrison (1773–1841) was the ninth president of the United States. He took office in March 1841 and died one month later. Earlier, he was a U.S. Army general. His most famous battles were the Battle of Tippecanoe (1811) and the Battle of the Thames (1813).

Sam Houston (1793–1863) led American troops in the Texas Revolution for independence from Mexico. In the revolution's final victory, Houston defeated Mexicans under General Santa Anna in the Battle of San Jacinto (1836). Then he became the first president of the Texas Republic.

Thomas Jefferson (1743–1826) was a plantation owner and member of the House of Burgesses. He wrote the Declaration of Independence, adopted on July 4, 1776. Jefferson was the third president of the United States (1801–1809). Monticello is his home and plantation.

Robert E. Lee (1807–1870) led the Confederate army in the Civil War. He surrendered to Union general Grant in 1865.

Shirley MacLaine (1934–) is an actress and dancer. She won the Academy Award for best actress for her role in the movie *Terms of Endearment* (1983).

James Madison (1751–1836) is called the Father of the Constitution. He helped write the U.S. Constitution. He also made sure the constitution had a Bill of Rights. Madison was the fourth president of the United States (1809–1817).

John Marshall (1755–1835) served in the Revolutionary War and the Virginia House of Burgesses. He was the chief justice of the U.S. Supreme Court (1801–1835).

Cyrus McCormick (1809–1884) invented a machine to harvest grain crops in 1831. McCormick started the International Harvester company in Chicago, Illinois.

James Monroe (1758–1831) was the fifth president of the United States (1817–1825). Monroe (pictured above left) declared that Europeans could no longer build colonies in the Americas. This declaration is known as the Monroe Doctrine.

Pocahontas (1595?–1617) was a Powhatan Indian princess. Her name means "playful." She was a friend to the Jamestown colonists. Pocahontas (pictured above right) married John Rolfe, a tobacco planter.

Edgar Allan Poe (1809–1849) wrote many scary mystery stories and poems. He was born in Massachusetts. After becoming an orphan, he lived in Virginia.

Walter Reed (1851–1902) was a U.S. Army surgeon. He discovered that yellow fever was spread by mosquitoes. Walter Reed Army Hospital in Washington, D.C., is named after him.

Bill "Bojangles" Robinson (1878–1949) was an African-American dancer and actor.

George C. Scott (1926–1999) was a movie, television, and stage actor. His most famous movie was *Patton* (1970). He received an Academy Award for this role, but he refused the award. He did not like the fierce competition the awards created among actors.

Captain John Smith (1580?–1631) was a leader in the Jamestown colony. Legend says that Pocahontas saved him from death.

Zachary Taylor (1784–1850) was the twelfth president of the United States (1849–1850). He gained national fame as a soldier in the Mexican War (1845–1846).

Nat Turner (1800–1831) was a Virginia slave who led a slave revolt in 1831.

John Tyler (1790–1862) was the tenth president of the United States (1841–1845). During his presidency, Tyler annexed Texas into the United States.

Booker T. Washington (1856–1915) was the son of a slave woman and a white man. He became a teacher and author. Washington founded Tuskegee Institute in Alabama. It was devoted to teaching black students.

George Washington (1732–1799) led the Continental army in the Revolutionary War. He was elected the first president of the United States (1789–1797). Mount Vernon is Washington's home and plantation.

Woodrow Wilson (1856–1924) was the twenty-eighth president of the United States (1913–1921). He led the nation through World War I (1914–1918) and worked to set up the League of Nations.

Tom Wolfe (1931–) is a magazine writer and book author. His novel *The Right Stuff* tells about astronauts' lives. It was made into a successful movie.

State Symbols

State bird: Cardinal

State flower: American dogwood blossom

State tree: American dogwood

State dog: American fox hound

State insect: Tiger swallowtail butterfly

State fish: Brook trout

State beverage: Milk

State shell: Oyster shell

State dance: Square dance

State boat: Chesapeake Bay deadrise

State fossil: *Chesapecten jeffersonius*

State song: Virginia has no state song. "Carry Me Back to Old Virginia" was once the state song. In 1997, the state legislature voted to remove it.

State commemorative quarter: released October 16, 2000

Making Virginia French Toast Breakfast Sandwiches

A great way to serve Virginia ham!

Makes two servings.

INGREDIENTS:

2 eggs

1/4 cup milk

1/4 teaspoon cinnamon

1 teaspoon vanilla

4 slices bread

2 slices Virginia ham (other ham may be used instead)

Syrup

DIRECTIONS:

Preheat the oven to 450°F. Grease an oven-safe dish. Beat the eggs in a bowl. Add the milk, cinnamon, and vanilla and mix well. Dip two slices of bread into the egg mixture so that both sides are coated. Lay them side-by-side in the greased dish. Place a slice of ham on each slice of bread. Dip the other two bread slices into the egg mixture. Lay them over the ham. Bake for 15 to 20 minutes. Serve with syrup for extra flavor. Your breakfast sandwiches are ready to eat!

Want to Know More?

At the Library

Fradin, Dennis. *The Virginia Colony*. Danbury, Conn.: Children's Press, 1986.

Harrah, Madge. *My Brother, My Enemy*. New York: Simon & Schuster, 1997.

Hermes, Patricia. *The Starving Time: Elizabeth's Diary, Book Two, Jamestown, Virginia, 1609*. New York: Scholastic, 2001.

January, Brendan. *The Jamestown Colony*. Minneapolis: Compass Point Books, 2000.

Joseph, Paul. *Virginia*. Edina, Minn.: Abdo & Daughters, 1998.

Sirvaitis, Karen. *Virginia*. Minneapolis: Lerner, 1991.

On the Web

Commonwealth of Virginia
http://www.myvirginia.org/
For information on Virginia's history, government, economy, and land

Virginia History on the Internet
http://www.lva.lib.va.us/whatwedo/k12/vhr/index.htm
For links to Virginia history and culture sites

Virginia Is for Lovers
http://www.virginia.org
For more information on places to visit and Virginia's history and arts

Through the Mail

Library of Virginia
800 East Broad Street
Richmond, VA 23219
For information about Virginia's history

Secretary of the Commonwealth
P.O. Box 2454
Richmond, VA 23218
For information on Virginia's state government

Virginia Tourism Corporation
901 East Byrd Street
Richmond, VA 23219
For information on travel and interesting sights in Virginia

On the Road

Virginia State Capitol
Broad Street
Richmond, VA 23219
804/698-1788

Index

About the Author

Ann Heinrichs grew up in Fort Smith, Arkansas, and lives in Chicago. She is the author of more than sixty books for children and young adults on Asian, African, and U.S. history and culture. Ann has also written numerous newspaper, magazine, and encyclopedia articles. She is an award-winning martial artist, specializing in t'ai chi empty-hand and sword forms.

Ann has traveled widely throughout the United States, Africa, Asia, and the Middle East. In exploring each state for this series, she rediscovered the people, history, and resources that make this a great land, as well as the concerns we share with people around the world.